Movie Jokes

Joe King

Abdo Kids Junior
is an Imprint of Abdo Kids
abdobooks.com

Abdo
ABDO KIDS JOKES
Kids

abdobooks.com

Published by Abdo Kids, a division of ABDO, P.O. Box 398166, Minneapolis, Minnesota 55439.

Printed in the United States of America, North Mankato, Minnesota.

052023

092023

THIS BOOK CONTAINS RECYCLED MATERIALS

Photo Credits: Alamy, Everett Collection, Getty Images, Shutterstock

Production Contributors: Teddy Borth, Jennie Forsberg, Grace Hansen

Design Contributors: Candice Keimig, Pakou Moua

Library of Congress Control Number: 2022946709

Publisher's Cataloging-in-Publication Data

Names: King, Joe, author.

Title: Movie jokes / by Joe King

Description: Minneapolis, Minnesota : Abdo Kids, 2024 | Series: Abdo kids jokes | Includes online resources and index.

Identifiers: ISBN 9781098266080 (lib. bdg.) | ISBN 9781098266783 (ebook) | ISBN 9781098267131 (Read-to-me ebook)

Subjects: LCSH: Jokes--Juvenile literature. | Wit and humor--Juvenile literature. | Motion pictures--Juvenile literature. | Humor--Juvenile literature.

Classification: DDC 818.6--dc23

Table of Contents

Movie Jokes

Where do mermaids see movies?

At the dive-in!

What did the trees think of the romantic comedy?

They thought it was too sappy!

What do cows do for fun?

They go to the mooooo-vies!

Why was Dorothy confused when she saw the Wicked Witch of the West and Glinda together?

She couldn't tell which witch was which!

Who gave the Wizard of Oz warts?

The Yellow Brick Toad.

What happened to the minions between *Despicable Me* and *Despicable Me 2*?

They Gru up.

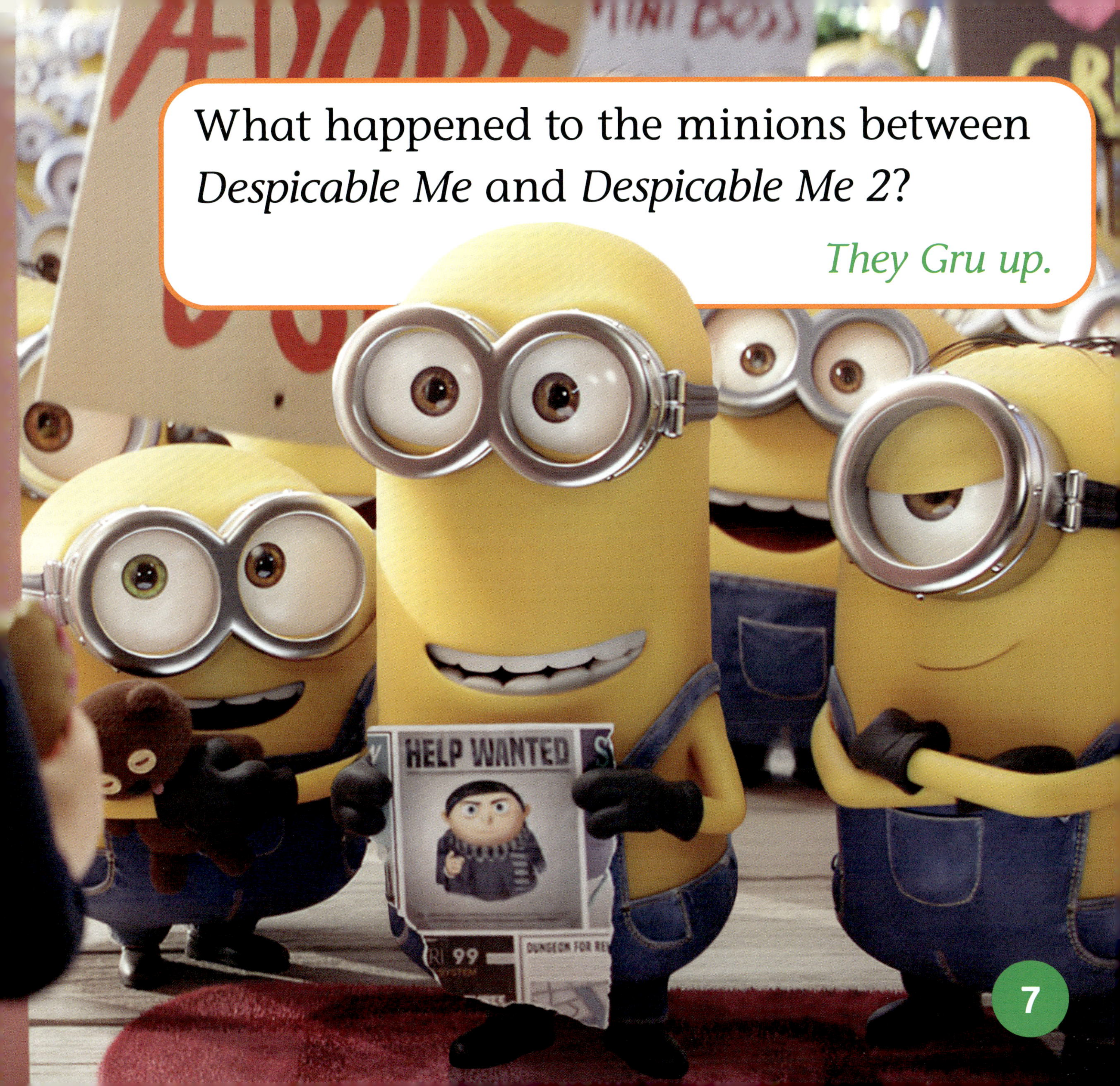

Did you hear about the Minecraft movie?

It's a blockbuster!

Why did King Kong climb the Empire State Building?

He couldn't fit in the elevator.

Why was Shrek upset when he got 500 new followers?

They all had torches and pitchforks!

Why was Cinderella
so bad at soccer?

She kept running away from the ball!

Why can't you give
Elsa a balloon?

She will let it go.

Why does Peter Pan always fly?
He can Neverland!
His jokes never land either!

Why is Spiderman so good at baseball?

He knows how to catch flies.

What superhero likes to cook?

Souper-man!

Have you seen *The Avengers* movie?

It was MARVELous!

I THOROughly enjoyed it!

What kind of cereal do they serve at Hogwarts?

Hufflepuffs.

How does Albus get into Hogwarts?

Through the Dumble-door.

You don't get my Harry Potter jokes?

There must be something RON with you.

Where's the invisibility cloak when you need it?!

What does Buzz Lightyear like to read?

Comet books!

What do you say to Simba when he's walking too slow?

Mufasta!

Why was King Triton angry over Ariel's report card?

Her grades were under the C.

What does Princess Leia say after she plants a tree?

May the forest be with you.

What do you call Chewbacca when he has chocolate stuck in his hair?

Chocolate chip wookiee.

How does Darth Vader like his toast?

On the dark side.

Why do stormtroopers always sleep with the lights on?

They are afraid of the Darth.

What did Obi-Wan say when Luke was having trouble using chopsticks?

"Use the fork, Luke."

Why did Star Wars movies come out in the order 4 5 6, 1 2 3 ?

In charge of the sequence, Yoda was.

Can we drive your Toyoda the rest of the way?

Joke-Telling Tips!

- Know your audience

- Timing is everything

- Confidence is key

- Go out on a high note!

Glossary

pun
a joke using a word that sounds like a different word or has another meaning. Examples from this book are "mufasta" (move faster and Mufasa) and "Gru up" (grew up).

romantic comedy
a movie genre that deals with love in a light and funny way.

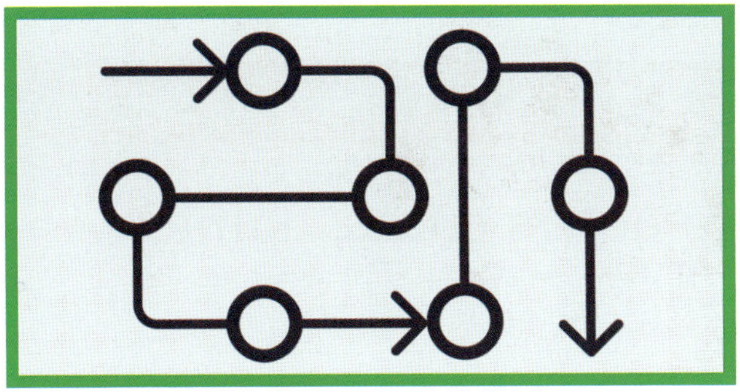

sequence
a pattern or process in which one thing follows another.

Index